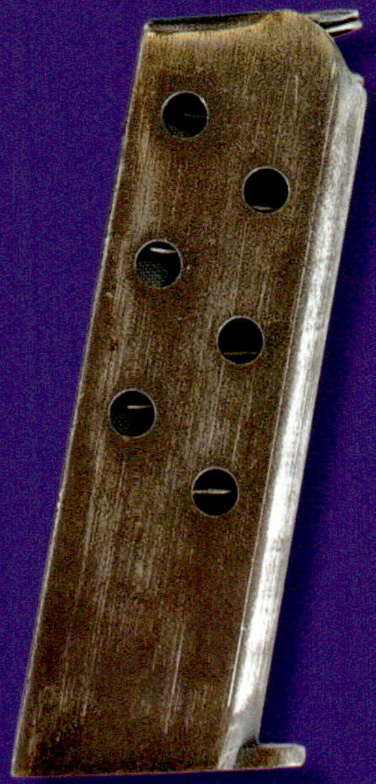

A 1910 FN Browning pistol was used to kill Archduke Ferdinand.

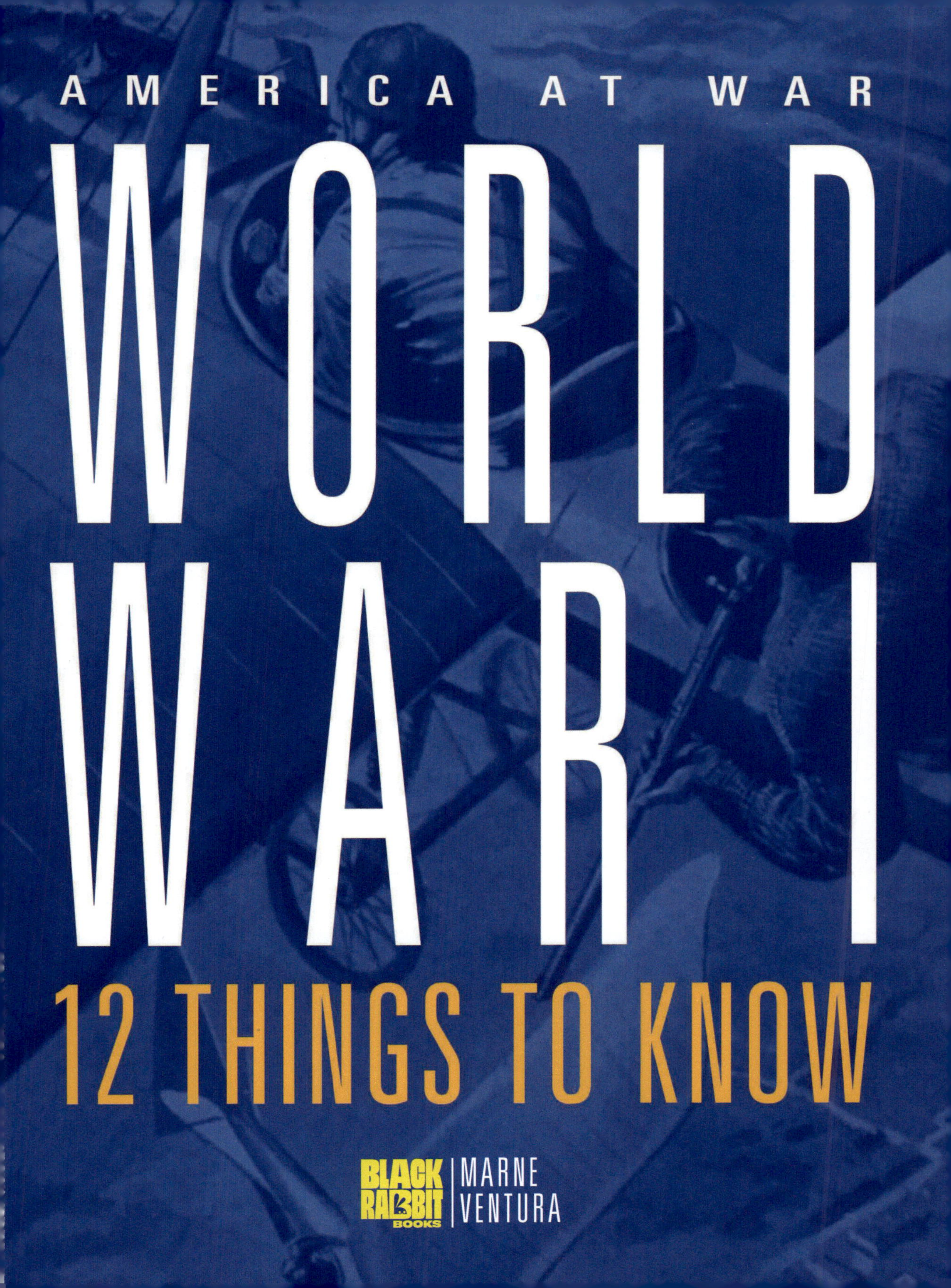

AMERICA AT WAR

WORLD WAR I

12 THINGS TO KNOW

BLACK RABBIT BOOKS

MARNE VENTURA

Table of Contents

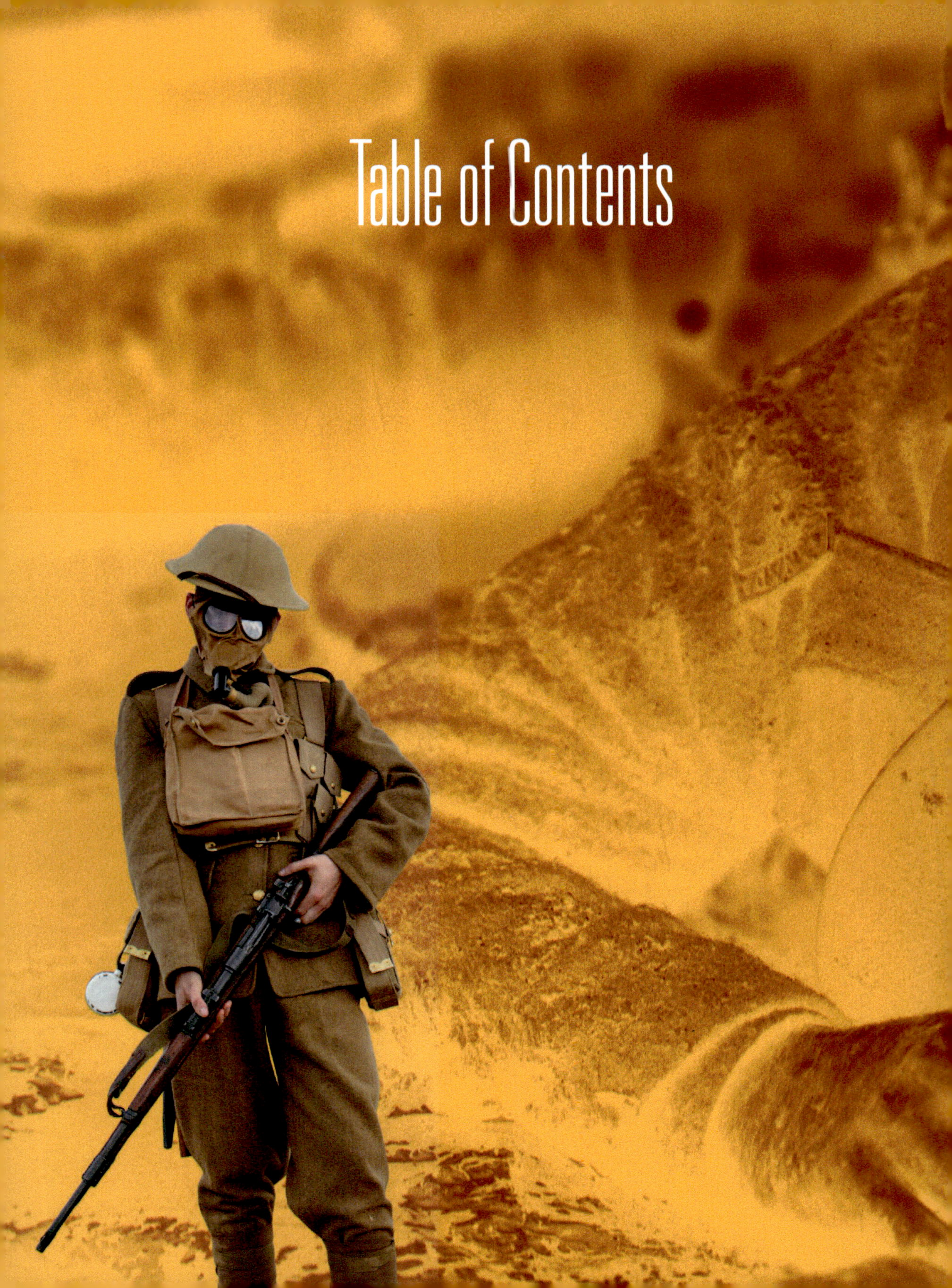

War to End All Wars *Begins*

1

The world changed forever on June 28, 1914. Archduke Franz Ferdinand, the heir to the Austria-Hungary throne, was **assassinated**. The man who killed him was from Bosnia-Serbia. He wanted to destroy the archduke's rule. This event would start World War I (1914–18).

Bosnia was a region in the south of Austria-Hungary. They wanted to be a free country. Serbia was their neighbor. They supported this decision. Serbia had been trying to unify the countries in southeastern Europe. They did not want to be part of Ferdinand's **empire**.

Austria-Hungary made up much of central Europe. Ferdinand's unexpected death threw the continent into chaos. Austria-Hungary

A stamp printed in Bosnia shows Archduke Franz Ferdinand.

declared war on Serbia. The rest of Europe had to choose sides. They were split into two groups. The Allies were the British Empire, France, Belgium, and Russia. Allies sided with Serbia.

The Central Powers were Germany, Austria, Hungary, Bulgaria, and Turkey. Germany was particularly worried about what might happen. Russia, France, and Great Britain surrounded its borders. Germans were afraid they would be overpowered. Austria-Hungary was its only chance for safety.

Many people thought the war would end by Christmas. But it lasted for four years. The United States wanted to stay **neutral**. But eventually, they would choose a side.

116,516 Total deaths of US soldiers in World War I.

About 4,735,000 US troops served in the war. • WWI was the largest war that the world had seen at the time. • About 8 million soldiers and sailors died. Another 20 million were injured.

The archduke and his wife were shot in Sarajevo, Bosnia.

United States Declares War *on Germany*

2

The first battle took place on August 4, 1914. German troops defeated Belgium. More fighting followed. British and French soldiers fought Germans in September. The battle was near the border of France and Belgium. A **boundary** for control formed. It was called the Western **Front**. The Western Front was around 475 miles (764 kilometers) long.

Across the continent, Russia attacked Germany and Austria-Hungary. This line of attack was called the Eastern Front. It was 1,000 miles (1,609 km) long. No one on either front seemed to be winning. But the fighting stretched on for years.

American citizens did not want to go to war. But January 1917 changed things. Germany had an **ambassador** in Mexico. He got a coded message.

A periscope in a German U-Boat submarine watches a battle.

29 Number of submarines in the German navy in 1917.

America also declared war on Austria-Hungary. It was official on December 7, 1917. • The Germans thought they could win the war before US troops got to Europe. • German subs sank several US ships in 1917.

The message was called the Zimmermann **Telegram**. The British got it first. They figured out what it said. The message asked Mexico to attack the United States. Germany promised to protect Mexico. This angered many Americans.

Then Germany did something else. On January 31, 1917, they put their submarines on offense. They would sink any ships around Great Britain. That included US ships. This threat was an act of war. President Woodrow Wilson could not stand by any longer. The United States declared war on Germany on April 6, 1917. It joined the Allies in fighting.

NAMING THE WAR At first, Americans called the conflict the European War. People thought it was the war to end all wars. When America joined the fight, it was known as "The World War." But many still called it the Great War. In 1941, a new war began. President Franklin D. Roosevelt called it the Second World War. It caught on. The public started calling it World War II.

United States Prepares *for War*

3

The United States was not ready for war. Their fighting force was small. In April 1917, there were only 200,000 trained men. That was both the regular army and the **National Guard**. Military leaders said it would take 1 million soldiers to win the war.

President Wilson and his advisers had a plan. They would hold a draft. On May 18, 1917, Congress passed the Selective Service Act. All men between the ages of 21 and 31 had to register. Men on the list were chosen at random. If picked, they would have to join the army.

General John Joseph Pershing

John J. "Black Jack" Pershing was a military man. He had served in the Spanish American War. He had also fought in Mexico. President Wilson chose him to lead in Europe. His army would be called the American Expeditionary Forces (AEF).

Pershing left for Great Britain on May 28, 1917. From there, he traveled to France. The French were happy to see him. By then, they were tired. The war had been going on for years. They hoped American soldiers would bring it to an end.

The first AEF troops arrived in France on June 26, 1917. Many of the soldiers were untrained. But this did not seem to matter. The men marched in a July 4 parade in Paris. Local people crowded the streets. They cheered, "Long live the Americans! Long live Pershing! Long live the United States!"

"Long live the
Long live Pers
Long live the

4,000 Number of AEF troops who landed in France on June 26, 1917.

The soldiers were called the First Provisional Division. • They arrived in the port of St. Nazaire. • Their arrival boosted French **morale**.

AEF troops march in a parade in Paris as Americans join the war.

Americans!
hing!
United States!"

US Soldiers Train *for War*

4

The new US soldiers did not go straight to the front lines. They needed to train. It took months to get them ready. The troops learned how to shoot and salute. And, most importantly, they learned how to fight.

General Pershing thought they would not be ready until 1919. The British and French military leaders could not wait. They needed the US troops to join French and British units on the front lines right away. But Pershing refused to break up his forces. He said his soldiers must go into battle as one. There would be no sending some to Britain and some to France.

Some experienced soldiers were nearly ready. They were part of the First Division. They were sent to Normandy, France, in June 1917. They spent 10 days on the frontlines. The French 18th Division showed them

A British sergeant major teaches US soldiers about bayonet charging.

650,000 Number of US soldiers expected in France by July 1918.

The first Americans were killed in action on November 3, 1917. • The area was believed to be a quiet combat zone. • Germans attacked. Three men died. Eleven were taken as prisoners.

trench warfare. Then, the men were rotated out. Others took their place. The First Division took part in their first trial on the front lines in October.

THINK ABOUT IT

US soldiers who arrived in France had a lot to learn. What were some of the skills they needed to survive? Which skill do you think was most important?

Americans Jump into *the Trenches*

5

World War I became famous for trench warfare. It was common on the Western Front. Each side dug deep ditches along the boundary. They were long and narrow. The area between the trenches was called "no man's land."

Trenches were not pleasant. They were full of rats. Soldiers stayed there for weeks at a time. They were always too cold or too hot. When it rained, they filled with filthy water. Many soldiers became ill. The trenches were dangerous too. In some places, the two sides were so close that grenades could be thrown back and forth. Or poisonous gas was used. Soldiers also mounted attacks. They climbed over the edge and tried to cross no man's land. They were usually gunned down. Many died. Neither side gained any ground.

Soldiers wore masks that protected them from poison gas.

The winter of 1917 was long and cold. More Americans came to fight. They trained. But neither side gained much ground. General Pershing did not agree with trench warfare. His troops were trained to attack and defend. The trenches were a European way of fighting. He did not think it could win a war. War on the Western Front **stalled** in 1917.

German stick grenade

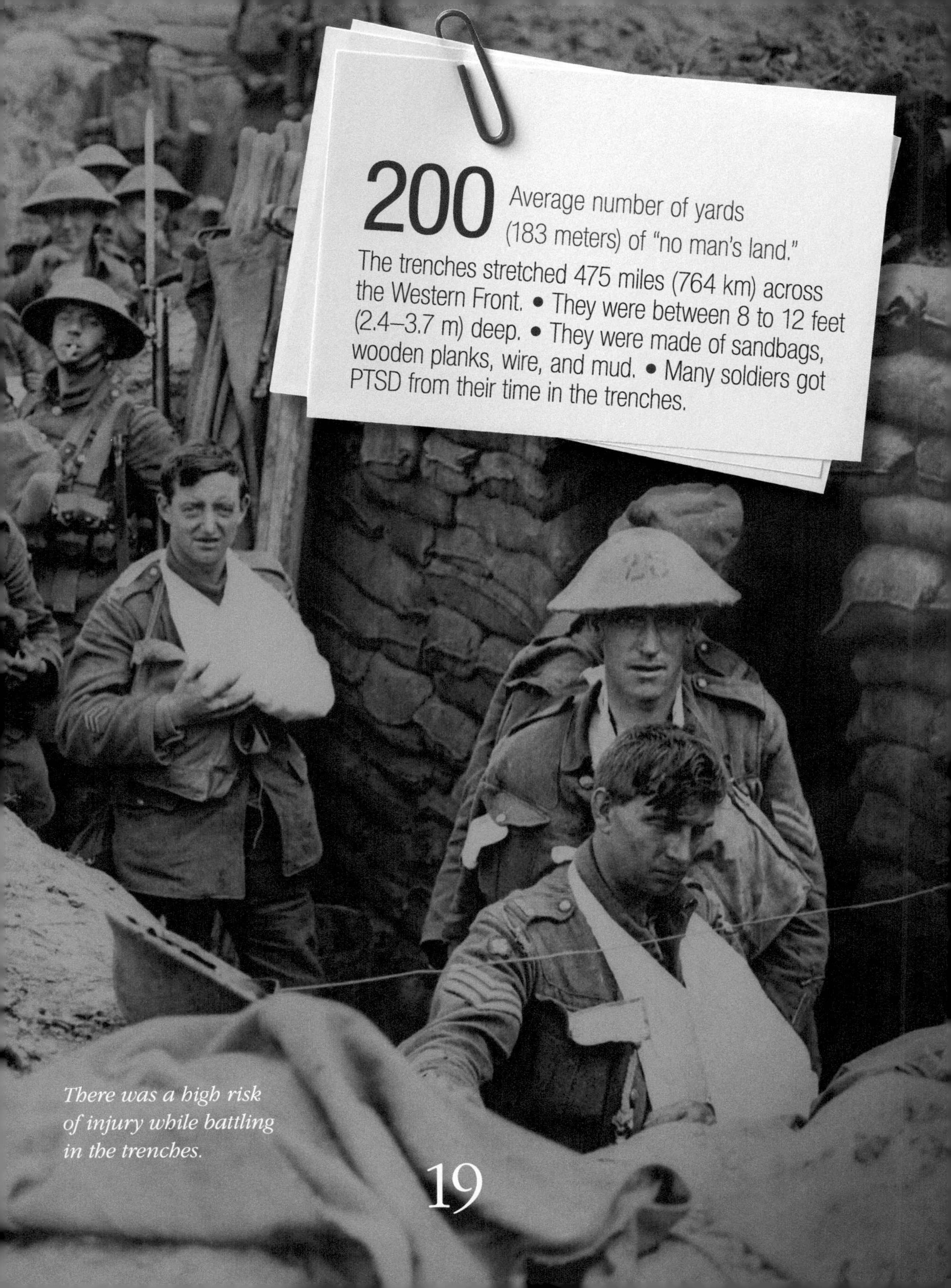

200 Average number of yards (183 meters) of "no man's land."

The trenches stretched 475 miles (764 km) across the Western Front. • They were between 8 to 12 feet (2.4–3.7 m) deep. • They were made of sandbags, wooden planks, wire, and mud. • Many soldiers got PTSD from their time in the trenches.

There was a high risk of injury while battling in the trenches.

STORMTROOPERS

Stormtroopers were **elite** German soldiers. They had special training. They could break through weak points in the Allied lines. Stormtroopers moved quickly and with very little gear. They fought with many different weapons. One was the first lightweight machine gun.

German Army Pushes toward *Paris*

6

In 1917, Russia withdrew from the war. Until then, the German army had been divided between the two fronts. Now, Germany could move its Eastern Front soldiers. They went to the Western Front.

On March 21, 1918, Germany attacked. They were northeast of the Somme River in France. Their poison gas shells flew into the British front lines. The British forces fell back. This was the first of five attacks that spring and summer.

The German attacks were successful at first. British and French forces gave up ground. The front lines gradually moved toward Paris. Allied leaders were desperate. They needed the help of US troops. But the Americans were still training. Some had trained in the trenches. But none had fought in a full-on battle. Pershing would not let his troops enter heavy combat zones until they were fully trained. By May 1, 1918, he had half a million soldiers in France.

The Germans kept attacking. The Allied forces kept falling back. Finally, Pershing saw that Paris could fall. It was time for his men to go to the Western Front.

500,000 Number of German troops that moved from the Eastern Front to the Western Front.

Germany and Russia signed a **truce** in December 1917. • Russian losses in the war played a role in causing the Russian Revolution. • Russian forces leaving left a big gap in the Allied defense.

GAS ATTACKS

WWI is known for **chemical warfare**. It is the first time dangerous gases were used on a large-scale attack. The gases made it hard to breathe. Soldiers wore masks. But they did not give full protection. One gas is known as mustard gas. It causes blisters and blindness. If breathed in, it causes shortness of breath. It damages the lungs and other organs.

The American, British, French, and German armies all had different style masks.

Americans Join the Fight to Stop *German Advance*

7

US General Pershing had the troops to help win the war. But the men were untested. They needed to prove themselves. On May 28, 1918, the US Army 28th Infantry moved into position. Their mission was to attack and take Cantigny. This was a city north of Paris, France.

The attack was a success. But the price was huge. The battle lasted three days. The French heavy **artillery** only helped during the first part. Then they were needed somewhere else. This left the US troops open to attack. The Germans used that to their advantage. About 200 US officers and men were killed or missing. Another 669 were wounded.

In June, French and American soldiers fought against the Germans in two major battles. They were bloody

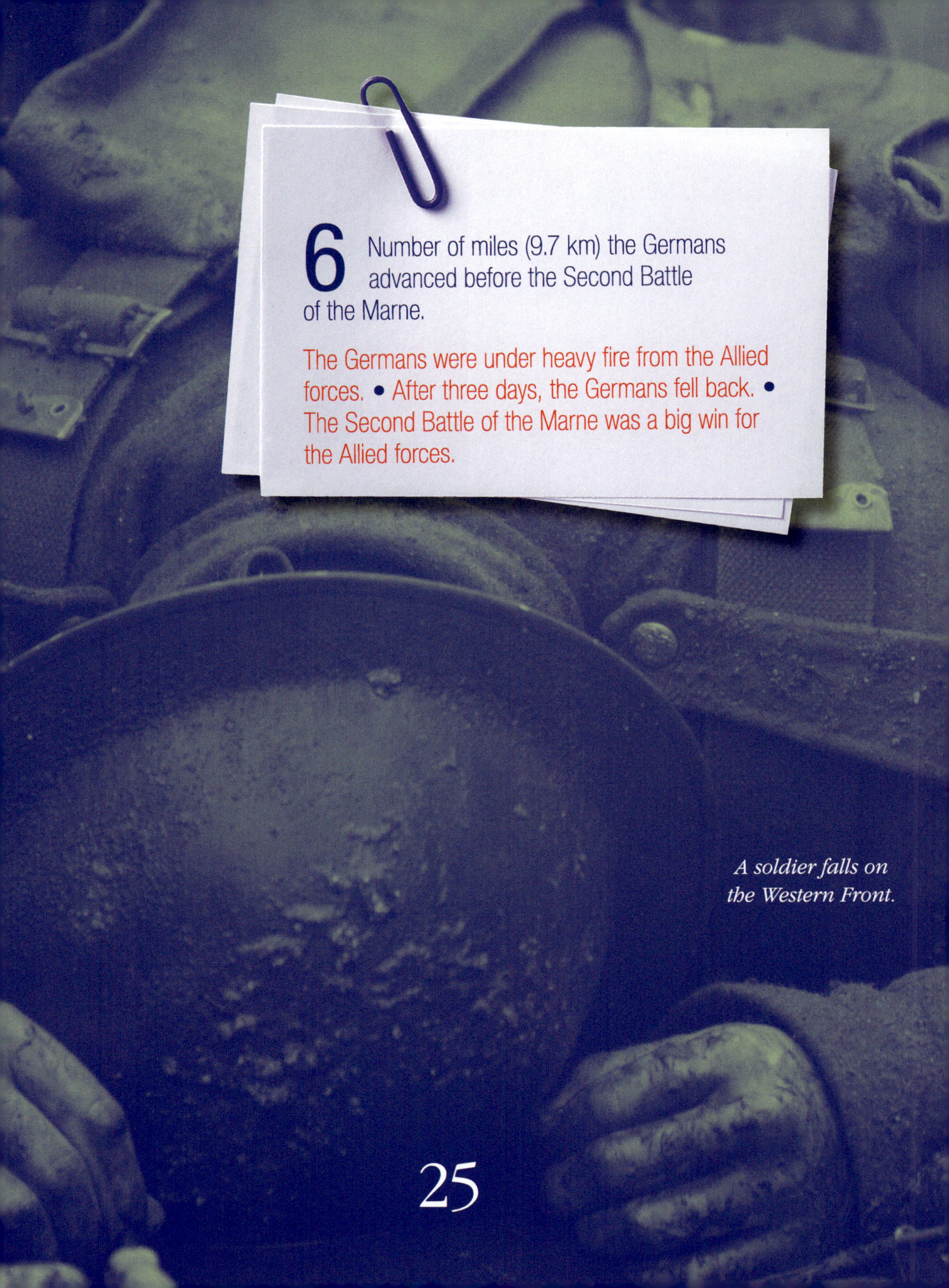

6 Number of miles (9.7 km) the Germans advanced before the Second Battle of the Marne.

The Germans were under heavy fire from the Allied forces. • After three days, the Germans fell back. • The Second Battle of the Marne was a big win for the Allied forces.

A soldier falls on the Western Front.

fights. Sometimes, the men had to fight in hand-to-hand combat. In the end, though, the Allies won.

The Second Battle of the Marne began on July 15, 1918. This was the fifth and final of the German spring attacks. The Allies fought hard. By July 20, the Germans began to fall back to the east. It was the beginning of the end of the war for Germany.

A statue honors the fallen during the battles of La Marne.

Air War Rages over France *and Germany*

8

WWI was also a battle of the skies. Both sides used planes for fighting. At first, pilots flew over the battlefields. They spied on enemies and dropped small bombs. Later, machine guns were mounted on the planes. The first air battle took place in 1915.

The United States did not have its own planes in Europe. American pilots flew French planes. Early in the war, Germans had more and better planes. Over time, Allied pilots built newer planes. They also gained more experience.

New fighter planes had just one pilot. They fought fierce battles in the sky. The battles were called "dogfights." Pilots from both sides fired machine guns at each other. Men who were very skilled at shooting down enemy planes were called "aces."

THINK ABOUT IT

Compare aircraft from WWI to fighter jets used today. How are they similar and different?

The "Red Baron" flew a Fokker Triplane, making it a popular plane for German pilots.

The most famous German ace was Manfred von Richthofen. He was known as the "Red Baron." A hero in Germany, he shot down 80 planes. He was killed on April 21, 1918. Before he died, he wrote down his story. The *Red Air Fighter* inspired other young pilots.

US ace Captain Eddie Rickenbacker was a former race car driver. He shot down 26 enemy planes. No other American pilot could match him. Rickenbacker survived the war. He wrote his own story. *Fighting the Flying Circus* was published in 1919.

Captain Eddie Rickenbacker

27 Captain Eddie Rickenbacker's age when he became a pilot.

Rickenbacker used his skills as a race car driver to become a fighter pilot. • He personally checked his aircraft, engine, guns, and bullets before each flight. • He was a member of the 94th Aero Squadron. Their logo was Uncle Sam's hat inside a ring.

Germans Yield Ground Slowly *as They Retreat*

9

At the end of July 1918, General Pershing had a plan. He shared it with Allied leaders who agreed. He set his plan in motion.

Pershing's troops traveled to northeast France. On September 12, 1918, they attacked at Saint-Mihiel. The Germans were surprised. They fell back. Pershing took many prisoners. The win gave the Allies confidence.

More German soldiers were in the northeast. They gathered in an area between the Meuse River and the Argonne Forest. Machine guns and cannons were ready to fire. Concrete bunkers protected the German troops. The Meuse-Argonne campaign began on September 26, 1918. The First Army had 600,000 men ready. They moved north. French, British, and Belgian forces launched similar attacks farther north along the front lines.

450 Number of German guns captured by the Americans.

It was the first American-led attack in WWI. • More than 1 million fresh US troops had arrived on the front lines. • It was the first major use of the US Army Air Service (later known as the US Air Force).

Americans open attack at the Battle of Saint-Mihiel.

General Pershing planned to capture a railway near Sedan, France. It would cut off the supply network to the German army. US troops used heavy artillery to destroy anything in their way. There was some confusion. Not all the new troops were organized. Mistakes were made. But there was no going back. It would be the bloodiest battle in the entire war.

In the end, the Allies were victorious. They reached the city of Sedan on November 9, 1918. WWI was almost over.

FAMOUS CARRIER PIGEON There were no modern radios during WWI. Instead, carrier pigeons took messages between units. On October 4, 1918, a US unit was trapped by the enemy. They sent out a carrier pigeon named Cher Ami. He carried a message for help. The Germans fired on Cher Ami, wounding him. Still, he flew 25 miles (40 km). He delivered the message and help was sent. Cher Ami was a hero.

US Army biplane

Germans Surrender to End *the Great War*

10

During the Meuse-Argonne battle, rumors began to fly. People said that peace talks were about to take place. By this time, everyone was sick of war. Both sides wanted to end the fighting.

Germany's leader was Kaiser Wilhelm II. He refused to consider a truce. On the warfront, Germany was losing ground. The flood of fresh US troops had tipped the scales in the Allies' favor. The Allies pushed the Germans back across the Western Front. In little time, the Germans lost most of their gains from the past four years.

Kaiser Wilhelm II of Germany

At home, the German people protested. They wanted to end the war. Crowds in the streets grew larger and louder. There was a threat of a revolution. On November 9, 1918, Wilhelm gave up. His supporters

10 million Estimated number of soldiers who died in WWI.

Each year, November 11 is a holiday in many Allied nations. • It is called Armistice Day in Europe. • It is called Veterans Day in the United States.

People in New York City hold newspapers announcing Germany's surrender.

were gone. The military was not on his side. He fled to Holland. New German leaders declared a **republic**. They agreed to a truce with the Allied Powers.

Early on November 11, 1918, representatives from both sides met in France. They signed an agreement. Fighting officially stopped at 11:00 a.m. that day. After four years, the end was in sight. But the war's impact would be felt for decades.

The Western Front (1914-1918)

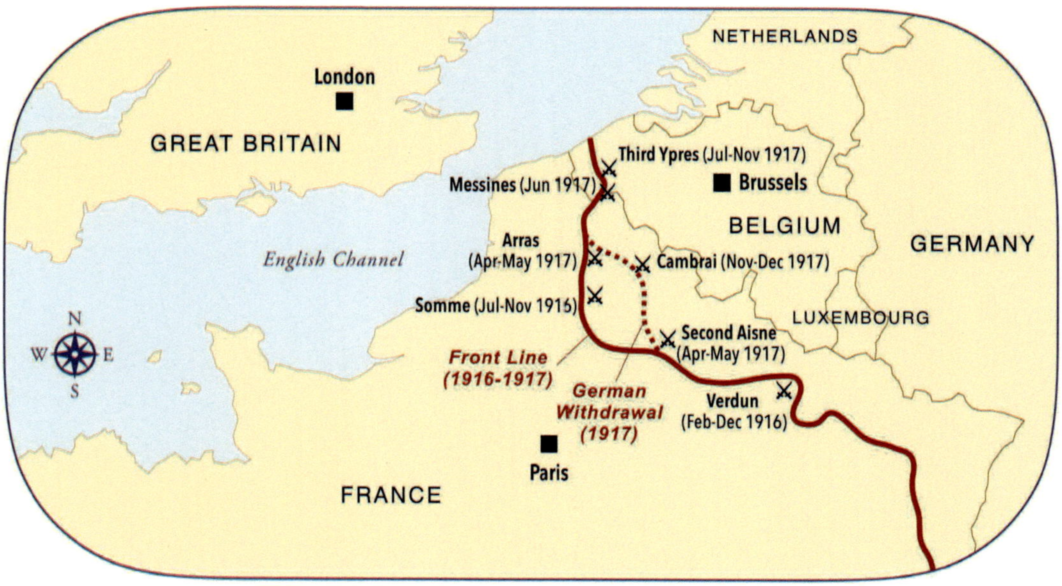

Paris Peace Conference *Brings Hope*

11

Though a truce had been reached, an official peace **treaty** still needed to be signed. On January 18, 1919, leaders met in Paris, France. It was known as the Paris Peace Conference. Three leaders took charge. They were American President Wilson, French Prime Minister George Clemenceau, and British Prime Minister David Lloyd George. Each man had different ideas about the peace terms.

English version of the Treaty of Versailles

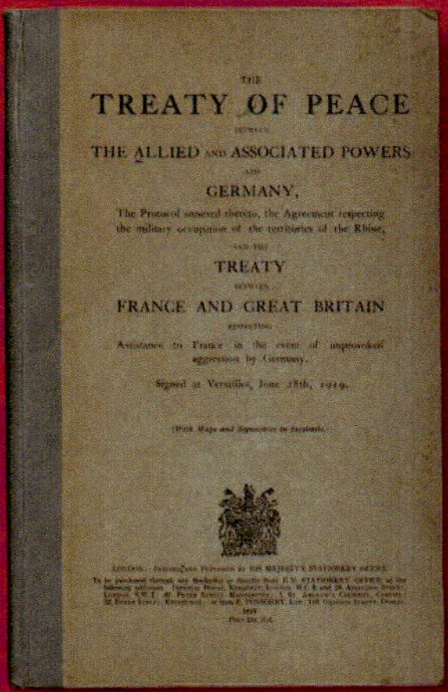

Clemenceau thought Germany should pay for the war. They should not have any power. Wilson called for a "just peace." The Germans would decide their own future. They could form their own government. George wanted a little bit of both. They all agreed on one thing. They would form a League of Nations. This was an international organization. It would try to solve problems between countries. Its goal was to maintain world peace. Its creation would lead to the United Nations.

Peace talks took place from January to June 1919. Germany was unhappy. It lost a large amount of land and natural resources. The country was also forced to pay for France to rebuild. Its colonies were given to other countries. The military was much smaller. But Germany was given no choice. If they did not agree, the war would keep going. On June 28, 1919, the Treaty of Versailles was signed.

The Treaty of Versailles was signed by representatives of 32 countries, including President Woodrow Wilson (far right).

TREATY SIGNED; WAR OVER

PRICE TWO CENTS.

The Evening World.

"Circulation Books Open to All."

NEW YORK, SATURDAY, JUNE 28, 1919.

14 PAGES

FINAL EDITION

PRICE TWO CENTS.

WILSON LEAVES PARIS; SAILS SUNDAY

GERMANS PLEDGED TO ACT IN GOOD FAITH

CITY'S BELLS RING TIDINGS AS PEACE TREATY IS SIGNED; FLEET JOINS IN CELEBRATION

JOY IN WALL STREET.

BEST DAY IN HISTORY SINCE BETHLEHEM, SAYS SECRETARY OF THE NAVY

TREATY SEVERE ON GERMANY, SAYS WILSON, BUT IMPOSES NOTHING SHE CANNOT DO

President in an Address to the American Public Says It Furnishes a Charter for a New Order and Ends Rule of Selfish Groups

GUNS BOOM, PLANES FILL AIR; FRENCH CROWDS CHEER PEACE

GERMANS PLEDGED TO ENFORCE TREATY; NO RESERVATION

WILSON, STARTING FOR HOME, BIDS FRANCE GODSPEED

Mueller Signs for Germans at 3.12, Bell a Minute Later—Wilson's Name Comes Next, Followed by Lloyd George and Clemenceau.

Soldiers Break Ranks and Join in the Demonstrations of Joy—Chinese Refuse to Attend Ceremony and Gen. Smuts Signs Under Protest.

VERSAILLES, June 28 (Associated Press).—The World War was formally ended to-day by the signing of the Peace Treaty with Germany.

The epochal meeting in the Hall of Mirrors began at 3.10 o'clock. The treaty was signed by Dr. Hermann Mueller at 3.12 o'clock (9.12 New York time) and by Johannes Bell at 3.13 P. M. They were followed by the American delegates, headed by President Wilson, and then by the plenipotentiaries of Great Britain, France, Italy and Japan. The representatives of the minor powers, signed in alphabetical order.

TREATY TERMS The terms for peace were harsh. Germany was to pull back all troops. It had to hand over military equipment. That included warships and submarines. Allied generals were not sure the new German government would accept the terms. They continued to plan like the war was still going.

Tensions Linger After *the War*

12

US soldiers went home after the treaty was signed. They were ready to go. They felt the military was too big. Too many people had lost their lives. The number of soldiers had peaked at 4.4 million in late 1918. By 1920, that number fell to 344,000.

France and Belgium had been torn apart by fighting. Many cities were destroyed. The people saw firsthand what war could do. All they wanted was peace. They wanted time to rebuild.

Allied leaders sat by and watched. Many had hoped the Treaty of Versailles would have been harsher. They wanted other countries to be afraid to lose. They wanted them to be too scared to ever try another war.

In Germany, citizens were angry. They felt the treaty was too harsh. Adolf Hitler became the German leader in 1933. He said his people's problems were because of the Treaty of Versailles. Under Hitler, Germany broke the terms of the treaty. They began to rebuild their military. US President Franklin D. Roosevelt warned world leaders about the broken terms. But they did not think there was much danger. No action was taken. With the Great War still fresh in memory, the Allies ignored Hitler. Tensions were high for another war.

Many photographs serve as a reminder of the horrors of war.

100,000 Number of soldiers the German army was limited to by the Treaty of Versailles.

The treaty banned Germany from drafting soldiers. • The German Navy was banned from owning submarines. • The treaty forced Germany to take the blame for starting WWI. They had to pay for damages.

The ghosts and ruins of the Great War left a lingering mark on many countries.

THINK ABOUT IT

General Pershing wanted to keep fighting. He wanted the German military to be crushed. Allied leaders rejected his suggestion. Why do you think they did not listen?

12 Key Dates

June 28, 1914
Archduke Franz Ferdinand is killed in Sarajevo, Bosnia and Herzegovina.

July 28, 1914
Austria-Hungary declares war on Serbia, beginning World War I.

April 6, 1917
The United States declares war on Germany.

June 26, 1917
The first US troops arrive in France.

November 3, 1917
The first US troops killed in combat.

March 21, 1918
Germany launches the first of five spring attacks.

June 28, 1914

April 6, 1917

March 21, 1918

May 28, 1918
Americans attack and take Cantigny, France.

September 12, 1918
The US First Army attacks at Saint-Mihiel.

September 26, 1918
The Meuse-Argonne campaign begins.

November 11, 1918
A truce agreement goes into effect at 11 a.m. Fighting officially stops.

January 18, 1919
The Paris Peace Conference begins.

June 28, 1919
The Treaty of Versailles is signed.

September 12, 1918

TREATY SIGNED; WAR OVER

The Evening World.

FINAL EDITION

WILSON LEAVES PARIS; SAILS SUNDAY

GERMANS PLEDGED TO ACT IN GOOD FAITH

BELLS RING TIDINGS PEACE TREATY IS SIGNED; FLEET JOINS IN CELEBRATION

BEST DAY IN HISTORY SINCE BETHLEHEM, SAYS SECRETARY OF THE NAVY

TREATY SEVERE ON GERMANY, SAYS WILSON, BUT IMPOSES NOTHING SHE CANNOT DO

President in an Address to the American Public Says It Furnishes a Charter for a New Order and Ends Rule of Selfish Groups

GUNS BOOM, PLANES FILL AIR; FRENCH CROWDS CHEER PEACE

GERMANS PLEDGED TO ENFORCE TREATY; NO RESERVATION

WILSON, STARTING FOR HOME, BIDS FRANCE GODSPEED

Mueller Signs for Germans at 3.12, Bell a Minute Later—Wilson's Name Comes Next, Followed by Lloyd George and Clemenceau.

Soldiers Break Ranks and Join in the Demonstrations of Joy—Chinese Refuse to Attend Ceremony and Gen. Smuts Signs Under Protest.

June 28, 1919

Glossary

ambassador
A person who represents his or her own government while living in another country.

artillery
Large guns used for land warfare.

assassinate
To kill another person, usually for pay or from loyalty to a cause.

boundary
An imaginary line where an area ends and another area begins.

chemical warfare
A war tactic that uses toxic chemicals as weapons.

elite
A select group that is superior in terms of ability or qualities.

empire
A large group of states or countries under one leader.

front
The line of contact of two opposing forces.

morale
A maintained belief in a goal or institution, especially during difficult times.

National Guard
The primary reserve military force in the United States.

neutral
Not connected with either side involved in a war.

republic
A state where power is held by the people and their elected representatives.

stall
To stop progressing.

telegram
A message sent over electrical wires and then printed out.

treaty
A formal agreement between two organizations or countries.

trench warfare
A type of land warfare using military trenches for shelter.

truce
An agreement between enemies or opponents to stop fighting for a certain time.

For More Information

Books

Adamson, Thomas K. *World War I.* Parker: The Child's World, 2024.

Medina, Nico. *What Was World War I?* New York: Penguin Workshop, 2023.

Monroe, Alex. *World War I.* Minneapolis: Bellwether Media, Inc., 2024.

Websites

Date Which Will Live in Infamy
education.nationalgeographic.org/resource/date-which-will-live-infamy

The United States Enters World War I
tpt.pbslearningmedia.org/resource/amex29gw-soc-usaenters/the-united-states-enters-world-war-i-american-experience

World War I
kids.britannica.com/kids/article/World-War-I/353933

About the Author

Marne Ventura is a children's book author and a former elementary school teacher. She holds a master's degree in education with an emphasis in reading and language development from the University of California.

Index

TOP RANK is published by Black Rabbit Books, P.O. Box 227, Mankato, MN, 56002.

• Designed by Danny Nanos • Photographs © Alamy Stock Photo/KEYSTONE Pictures USA, 38, Shawshots, 41, Trains and Planes, 33; Dreamstime/Andrew Oxley, 27, James Kirkikis, 27; Shutterstock/Belinda Pretorius, 48, Brendan McCartney, 40, De Jongh Photography, 26, Dimitrios Karamitros, 36, Everett Collection, cover, 1, 18–19, 22–23, 35, 37, 42–43, Hedley Lamarr, 2–3, 24–25, irin-k, 17, JakeOwenPowell, 4, 18, Jolygon, 46–47, Olemac, 21, Olga Popova, 5, Pavel L Photo and Video, 2, 17, Simon Vandamme, 28–29, 45, spatuletail, 10; Wikimedia Commons/Achille Beltrame, 7, 44, American official photographer / Imperial War Museums, 42, Auckland War Memorial Museum Tamaki Paenga Hira, 37, Bain News Service / Library of Congress, 11, Cassowary Colorizations, 14–15, 16, 20, 44, Department of Defense. Department of the Army. Office of the Chief Signal Officer, 39, Harris & Ewing, 13, 29, Kallen2021, 39, 45, Lucien Hector Jonas, 31, 45, Morio, 32, National Museum of the U.S. Navy, 9, The U.S. National Archives, 10, 44, Thomas Heinrich Voigt, 34

Library of Congress Cataloging-in-Publication Data: Names: Ventura, Marne author | Title: World War I: 12 things to know / by Marne Ventura. | Other titles: World War One | Description: Mankato, MN: Top Rank is an imprint of Black Rabbit Books, [2026] | Series: America at war | Includes bibliographical references and index. | Audience term: juvenile | Grades 4–6 | Ages 9–13 | Identifiers: LCCN 2024050103 | ISBN 9781644668269 (library binding) | ISBN 9781644668580 (paperback) | ISBN 9781644668900 (ebook) | Subjects: LCSH: World War, 1914-1918—Miscellanea—Juvenile literature | Classification: LCC D522.7 .V46 2026 | DDC 940.53—dc23/eng/20241121 | LC record available at https://lccn.loc.gov/2024050103